Also available in this series from Quadrille:

MINDFULNESS
MINDFULNESS II
QUIET
FRIENDSHIP
LOVE
CONFIDENCE
TIDINESS
HAPPINESS
MOTHERHOOD
LUCK
US
SEX
CHRISTMAS
SELF-CARE

the little book of
SISTERHOOD

Hardie Grant

QUADRILLE

Sisterhood

Definition:
noun

1. a: The state of being a sister
   b: Sisterly relationship

2. A community or society of sisters

3. The solidarity of women based on shared conditions, experiences or concerns

We may not have it all together,
but together we have it all.

Women don't need to have the same experience of womanhood to come together as part of the sisterhood.

- Masculine
- Androgynous
- Feminine
- CEO
- Stay-at-home mother
- Carer
- Volunteer
- Entrepreneur
- Unemployed
- Etc.

Stop fighting.

Start working together.

Being part of a sisterhood
means never being alone.

Supportive

Inspiring

Sustaining

Truthful

Energizing

Robust

Honourable

Open

Opinionated

Divine

The sisterhood transcends class, culture, colour, creed, prejudice and preference.

There is not one experience of what it means to be a woman.

Listen to the experiences of women different to yourself and try to take something new and learned away from the conversation.

English: Sisterhood

Finnish: *Sisarkunta*

German: *Schwesternschaft*

Hungarian: *Apácarend*

Portuguese: *Irmandade*

Slovak: *Sesterstva*

Spanish: *Hermandad*

Turkish: *Kardeşlik*

Welsh: *Chwaeroliaeth*

"Help[ing] one another is part of the religion of our sisterhood."

LOUISA MAY ALCOTT

Sisterhood exists wherever there is female relationship and friendship:

- Sisters
- Mothers and daughters
- Grandmothers and granddaughters
- Aunts and nieces
- Cousins
- Friends
- Teachers and students
- Mentors and guides
- You and the future of womankind

Behind every successful woman
is a tribe of other women who
have her back.

"Women who understand how powerful they are do not give into envy over meaningless things, instead they fight to maintain the beautiful bond of the sisterhood. These are the real women who know that we need each other's love and support to survive in this world. Love is the essence of being a woman. We must be that light of love that seals the bond and unique beauty of our sisterhood."

BINDU

Life becomes a little easier to navigate when women support each other.

To be a sister is to:

- Communicate
- Share a hug
- Forgive
- Help out
- Be loyal
- Soothe
- Be there, come what may

"Women are a sisterhood. They make common cause in behalf of the sex; and, indeed, this is natural enough, when we consider the vast power that the law gives us over them."

WILLIAM COBBETT

The sisterhood is sewn together with small acts of kindness.

"This is not a letter but my arms around you for a brief moment."

KATHERINE MANSFIELD

Never underestimate how deeply others will appreciate your kindness.

The sisterhood finds inspiration from women of all backgrounds

The East Prussian artist Käthe Kollwitz (1867–1945) has created some of the most heartbreaking sculptures of women and children shattered by war. She expressed the universality of suffering, and looked outside conventional ideas of behaviour and beauty.

Muslim women will sometimes greet each other as "sister" and women are encouraged to avoid gossiping about each other, to be hospitable and to uphold ties of kinship.

"The working-class woman shows me much more than the ladies who are totally limited by conventional behaviour. The working-class woman shows me her hands, her feet, and her hair. She lets me see the shape and form of her body through her clothes. She presents herself and the expression of her feelings openly, without disguises."

KÄTHE KOLLWITZ

Sisters before misters.

Sisterhood does not:

- Elevate female beauty over female goodness

- Prioritize superficial appearance over meaningful kindness

- Value looks over personality

"It is amazing how complete is the delusion that beauty is goodness."

LEO TOLSTOY
The Kreutzer Sonata

#sisterhood

#girlpower

#sisterhoodispowerful

#persisterhood

#sisterlove

#BBF4EVA

#friends4forlife

#womensupportingwomen

Days to honour the sisterhood:

- International Women's Day: 8 March
- Women's History Month: March
- Mothering Sunday: fourth Sunday of Lent (UK), second Sunday of May (US)
- Girl Friends Day: 1 August
- Single Working Women's Day: 4 August
- Women's Equality Day: 26 August
- National Sister's Day: first Sunday of August
- Mother-in-law Day: 27 October

Sisterhood = all women.

Where to hang out with the sisterhood online:

Mumsnet: Launched in 2000, it is the go-to forum for all things baby, family and work/life balance related. With over 10,000 bloggers and social-media influencers involved, it's a one-stop portal for parents.

Skillshare: The sisterhood is nothing if not massively into the concept of sharing. Join the American online learning community to access 27,000 premium and 2,000 free courses from experts on everything from how to tattoo to sugarcraft.

Theglasshammer: Sponsored by Goldman Sachs and PWC, among others, The Glasshammer is a "career resource for professional women" providing "coaching and networking opportunities to empower you as you navigate your path at work".

While there is no official law book of **The Girl Code**, somehow women know the rules without being taught them. If you're not sure, here's a short refresher...

Do:

- Support your friend in everything she's trying to achieve

- Be honest if your friend asks if she isn't looking her best

- Alert your friend to wardrobe malfunctions

- Share with each other

Don't:

- Be harsh

- Compare and criticize your friend

- Undermine your friend

- Spill your friend's secrets

Sisterhood must be built on a solid foundation of humour, silliness and shenanigans.

"Friendship is a serious affection; the most sublime of all affections, because it is founded on principle, and cemented by time."

MARY WOLLSTONECRAFT

The six seasons of sisterhood

Early girlhood: Defined by giggles, plaits/braids and pinafores, little girls band together to create vivid imaginative worlds of their own.

Later girlhood: Accompanied by laughter, learning and the first exploration of love, older girls form formidable unions.

Young women: Energized by spirited fun and hedonism, the sisterhood is the armour that young women wear as they explore the world. Friends are fellow adventurers.

Woman: Fully fledged as an individual with a career and independent home, women rely on the sisterhood for a deep broadening of experience.

Mother: Splattered with purée and exhausted with sleep deprivation, the sisterhood sustains mothers through this most intense of learning periods.

Wise woman: The summation of the sisterhood when relationships between women of different ages flourish and wisdom is passed down the generations.

"Walking with a friend in the dark is better than walking alone in the light."

HELEN KELLER

Think of the sisterhood as the gentle waves of an ocean, always present but lapping in and out of your life.

There are stages when the presence of the sisterhood will be stronger and weaker, where priorities lie elsewhere but you will still hear the gentle ocean song of the ever-present sisterhood. Walk to the ocean and dip in or dive in when you have the opportunity.

Pivotal moments when you need the sisterhood:

- Youthful exploration
- Caring for a first-born
- The school run
- Returning to work
- Catastrophe
- Empty nesting

The sisterhood has come full circle.

Traditional sisterhood rituals

The "red tent" or "moon hut": When girls began their menstrual cycles, some ancient communities would welcome the girls into a red tent or moon hut where older women would share their wisdom about womanhood as well as their fertility cycle.

Dancing to Artemis: In Ancient Greece, where the cult of Artemis was followed, young girls looked to the goddess to guide them into adulthood. At ritual sites, girls would dance to the goddess in order to win her favour in guiding them from their first period to their first childbirth.

Croning ceremony: To celebrate the time when women left their child-bearing years behind, some pagan communities staged croning ceremonies. Women would be honoured to mark their contributions of wisdom and knowledge.

Modern sisterhood rituals

The hen party: Ritual costumes (angel wings or learner plates) are worn by a bride during a pre-marital celebration. She is surrounded by a group of friends and female relations who imbibe intoxicating substances and engage with profane ritualistic items (chocolate penises). The hen party ritual begins at dusk and exact details about what happens are often tricky to establish.

The baby shower: Groups of women gather to give love, support and presents to a woman soon to give birth. Cake is eaten, advice about milk feeding is ignored and ritual offerings to the birthing goddess are opened (baby clothes and toiletries that the new mother will be too tired to use). Mature women agree to remain silent about precisely what this young woman is going to experience. No one mentions the perineum.

The girls' night in: Women lie around, either on sofas or beds, catching up and spending quality time together. Anthropologists are foggy about the exact purpose of this six-weekly ritual. Suggestions have been made that the event is convened as a cover to discuss other women not present at the ritual.

Being part of the sisterhood means you are surrounded by loving critics.

What's the collective noun
for a group of sisters?

A squabble.

Molly, my sister, and I fell out,
And what do you think it was about?
She loved coffee and I loved tea,
And that was the reason we could
not agree.

traditional folk nursery rhyme

Sisterhood should not let petty differences get in the way of good relations.

There is enough room for all women to be whole without tearing each other down.

The sisterhood is not a hall of mirrors. Do not enter hoping to see yourself reflected, to see heads nod when yours nods or heads shake when yours shakes.

No, the sisterhood is more like an enchanted forest whose delights will move your head in directions you didn't know were possible.

Toxic female myths to get over:

- Women don't support women

- Women actively hate women

- Women bosses are horrible to other women

- Women are more interested in men than friends

- Women lack confidence to lead

- Women are bitchy

Think carefully about using gendered insults when describing women.

Not everyone is perfect, but let's try our best not to insult each other.

Create a new way of thinking

Try not to judge one another, certainly not out loud, in a conspiratorial whisper or online.

Be kind, support and empower.

Within the sisterhood you will
find strong and weak characters.
Dominant and subservient women,
beautiful and intelligent females
and the plain and ordinary.

None of this matters.

At the heart of all decent sisterly
relationships is love. With love,
all chasms in beauty, strength
and experience can be bridged.

Brooke sisters

George Eliot's masterpiece
Middlemarch, 1871–2, tells the
story of down-to-earth Celia
and her lofty, idealistic sister
Dorothea Brooke, who, though
vastly different characters,
always support each other.

Celia and Dorothea Brooke
in *Middlemarch*

"As Celia bent over the paper, Dorothea put her cheek against her sister's arm caressingly. Celia understood the action. Dorothea saw that she had been in the wrong, and Celia pardoned her. Since they could remember, there had been a mixture of criticism and awe in the attitude of Celia's mind towards her elder sister. The younger had always worn a yoke, but is there any yoked creature without its private opinions?"

GEORGE ELIOT
Celia and Dorothea Brooke
in *Middlemarch*

Do:

- Do converse

- Do demonstrate loyalty

- Do empathize

Don't:

- Don't gossip
- Don't betray
- Don't gloat

Her success is not your failure.

"Do not tell secrets to those whose faith and silence you have not already tested."

QUEEN ELIZABETH I

Let's not deny that there is a certain element of competition between women and that healthy competition is of course a good thing. These sisters exemplify sisterly competition – good and bad...

Venus and Serena Williams

Seven-time Grand-Slam title winner Venus and her younger sister, 23 Grand-Slam title winner Serena, have driven women's tennis to new heights of sporting brilliance. While their on-court rivalry – facing each other in over 30 tournaments – has been nail-biting to watch, their sisterly affection off-court remains strong. Personally close, the sisters have won 22 titles when playing doubles together.

A. S. Byatt and Margaret Drabble

Authors Dame Antonia Susan Duffy (known professionally as A. S. Byatt) and her younger sister Margaret Drabble have pursued their sibling rivalry on and off the page. Margaret first achieved literary acclaim with her novels *A Summer Bird-Cage*, *The Millstone* and *Jerusalem the Golden* but was perhaps eclipsed by her sister's Booker-Prize-winning *Possession*. Margaret later penned *The Peppered Moth* where sibling competitiveness loomed large. The sisters, though not close, insist their feud has been widely over-blown.

Open and honest conversation
is at the heart of the sisterhood.

No one who has been on a hen weekend, contributed to a WhatsApp group or woken up after an all-girls sleepover can deny that the happiest of sisterhoods can be fraught with division, moods, irrational behaviour, attitude, irritability and frustration. And that's on a good day.

To avoid unnecessary arguments, try:

- Pausing before you respond

- Leaving the room

- Not to raise your voice (or type in CAPITALS)

- Not to take it to heart

The sisterhood is enriched when variety of thought is examined, different experiences are shared and prejudices (however virtuous) are shattered.

Try these easy tactics to help you navigate political polarization:

- Don't take different opinions personally

- Be curious about views that oppose your own

- Show interest in your friends' perspective

- Don't expect to change your friends' minds

- Take it offline

- Be reflective, not reactive

Embrace difference

It may hurt when friends produce children when you are childless, to celebrate their promotion while you are unemployed or to witness your dearest ally fall in love while you are happily single. At such crucial points, the closest of friendships can splinter into opposing directions. Do not let the fracture develop into a full break. Let it heal.

Fostering friends whose lives are being led at different speeds to your own will ultimately enrich, empower and embolden both parties.

*"I could never love anyone as
I love my sisters."*

LOUISA MAY ALCOTT

Host a family gathering

A great way to harvest the wisdom of the members of your sisterhood is to invite the female members of your family for a party. Suggest coffee, tea, lunch or supper, a picnic even – whatever suits you and works to provide a forum for friendly, open discussion.

"For there is no friend like a sister
In calm or stormy weather;
To cheer one on the tedious way,
To fetch one if one goes astray,
To lift one if one totters down,
To strengthen whilst one stands."

CHRISTINA ROSSETTI

Sisters are different flowers
from the same garden.

" You know full well as I do the value of sisters' affections: There is nothing like it in this world. "

CHARLOTTE BRONTË

" There can be no situation in life in which the conversation of my dear sister will not administer some comfort to me. "

LADY MARY WORTLEY MONTAGU
*The Letters and Works of
Lady Mary Wortley Montagu*

"Sisters are brittle things."

EMILY DICKINSON

Sisterhood leaves a legacy to future generations of fulfilling female relationships and feminine power.

The first girl group

Martha, Connee and Helvetia Boswell are often hailed as the first girl band. The close harmony group took America by storm in the 1930s. Classically trained with huge jazz and blues influences, The Boswell Sisters topped the American charts in 1935 with their hit "The Object of My Affection".

10 superb girl groups

- Spice Girls
- The Andrews Sisters
- TLC
- Destiny's Child
- AKB48
- The Pussycat Dolls
- Bananarama
- The Pointer Sisters
- The Nolans
- The Supremes
- En Vogue

Dashwood sisters

Both sisters are effectively dumped by noble Edward and the dastardly Mr Willoughby, and their reactions couldn't be more contrasting. Elinor keeps her heartbreak quiet while Marianne wails, loses her appetite and finally has a complete emotional and physical collapse. In each other's different responses, the sisters learn from one another about the necessity of both sense and sensibility.

Elinor and Marianne Dashwood
in Jane Austen's *Sense and Sensibility*

March sisters

Sensible, clever, pretty and loving, the March sisters in *Little Women* embody all that was thought to be worthy in the 19th-century version of womanhood. It's hard to be cynical when the girls react so heroically to the privations of the Civil War, love and loss.

Meg, Jo, Beth and Amy March
in Louisa May Alcott's *Little Women*

Bennet sisters

On the death of their father, all five Bennet girls will be evicted from their family home, so the race is on for them to marry well. Beautiful Jane, clever Lizzie, serious Mary and silly Kitty and Lydia, urged on by their embarrassing mother, set about the task of marrying with varying degrees of love and dignity.

Jane, Elizabeth, Mary, Catherine and Lydia Bennet in Jane Austen's *Pride and Prejudice*

Call the girls, open the wine, bring the tissues and watch:

- *Hannah and Her Sisters*: 1986
- *Beaches*: 1988
- *Steel Magnolias*: 1989
- *Thelma & Louise*: 1991
- *Bend It Like Beckham*: 2002
- *Charlie's Angels: Full Throttle*: 2003
- *Mamma Mia!*: 2008
- *Sex and the City*: 2008
- *The Secret Life of Bees*: 2008
- *Bridesmaids*: 2011
- *Bad Moms*: 2016

Wakefield twins

Fun-loving Jessica and serious Elizabeth are the perfect complement to each other as they adventure forth into the dramas and complications of high-school life. The 1983–2003 series was proof that readers can't get enough of tales of sisterly adventures.

Jessica and Elizabeth Wakefield
in Francine Pascal's *Sweet Valley High*

Charlotte, Emily and Anne Brontë

So close were the 19th-century Brontë sisters that they were believed to share the same imagination. Living amidst the wild Yorkshire moors, the Brontë sisters began writing from a young age and between them produced, among other literary achievements:

- *Jane Eyre* (Charlotte)
- *Wuthering Heights* (Emily)
- *The Tenant of Wildfell Hall* (Anne)

All of which are masterpieces of English literature.

Mitford sisters

Nancy, Pamela, Diana, Unity, Jessica and Deborah Mitford embody 20th-century history in six sisters. Nancy was the author of *Love in a Cold Climate*, Pamela a lover of the countryside, Diana and Unity were devotees of fascism, Jessica a member of the American Communist Party and Deborah became the Duchess of Devonshire and chatelaine of the magnificent Chatsworth House.

All writers or sensational diarists, these six siblings give lie to the notion that sisters are by nature and disposition similar.

> *"We secure our friends not by accepting favours but by doing them."*

THUCYDIDES

A sisterhood challenge

This week aim to be a good friend:

- Don't cancel because you're tired/can't be bothered/ have work to do.

- Do one special thing for one friend.

- Instead of "liking" a post, call or visit.

There is nothing more isolating for a woman than standing alone while another group of women are enjoying each other's company. Make proactive steps to be friendly.

Be welcoming to women who sit or stand alone.

" *There are many Beths in the world, shy and quiet, sitting in corners till needed, and living for others so cheerfully that no one sees the sacrifices till the little cricket on the hearth stops chirping, and the sweet, sunshiny presence vanishes, leaving silence and shadow behind.* "

LOUISA MAY ALCOTT
Little Women

The Women's Institute: Founded in 1915, the WI is the largest women's voluntary organization in the UK with nearly 220,000 members and over 6,000 branches. Based on the ideals of fellowship, truth, tolerance and justice, the WI is non-sectarian and non-party political. Meeting on a monthly basis, the Women's Institute offers a space for friendship, enrichment and campaigning. And many cups of tea and delicious pieces of cake.

One of the most powerful and beneficial experiences of the sisterhood is to experience cross-generational friendships. Fertilize each other by harvesting the wisdom of the old and the energy of the young.

Becoming part of the sisterhood is a declaration of intent

- You intend to support fellow sisters.

- You intend to embrace women who need help.

- You intend your values and wisdom to be used for the furtherance of the welfare of women.

- You intend to rely on other sisters when you need help, reassurance, comfort and the most belly-shaking laughs you will ever experience.

Sisterhood allows you to involve yourself in a long-term meaningful way in causes that advance the welfare and wellbeing of fellow sisters.

Be yourself

We live in a world that attempts to tell women how to exist. Remember to:

- Respect yourself
- Define womanhood for yourself
- Live a life that **you** are happy with

Michelle Obama

In 2009, Michelle Obama visited an all-girls school in Islington, London, where at least 20% of pupils were refugees and over 50 languages were spoken. After an emotional speech where the First Lady encouraged the students to aim high and support each other, she did not sweep out. No, Michelle Obama fostered the relationship with the school: she took some of the students to Oxford University to inspire their studies, invited others to the White House and revisited the school during her *Becoming* book tour in 2018.

During her final visit she encouraged the girls to practise the kind of sisterhood where they find strength in each other to overcome their doubts and naysayers.

M&M's game

Yellow: embarrassing moment
Red: romance
Green: travel
Brown: home life
Orange: shocking
Blue: wild card

Pass round a bag of M&M's and take it in turns to choose a sweet. Before eating, each sister has to share a story relating to the colour sweet she's chosen.

Balloon bang

Give each sister a piece of paper and a balloon. After writing one piece of information about herself on the paper, each sister inserts it into the balloon and blows it up. The balloons are then released into the room and popped, with the sisters working out which information belongs to whom.

Excuses to party with the sisterhood

- First kiss
- Best kiss
- Passing exams
- Failing exams
- Getting a job
- Losing a job
- Marriage
- Divorce

Your birthday

Her birthday

Her friend's birthday

- Her friend's friend's birthday

- It's the weekend

- It's nearly the weekend

- You just want to hang out

Three lovely ways to spend time with busy friends

Once school and college are completed, you may find that the wonderful lake of female friendships has suddenly evaporated. With careers and families to juggle, more structure is needed to nurture the sisterhood. These ideas work very well on a six-week basis...

Book club

Invite any readers you know (as many as can fit around a table), suggest a book to read, cook food and chat.

It works well if the woman who is hosting the event chooses the book. As the sessions unfold, conversations will take the participants to the mountains and valleys of life's landscape.

Cookery book club

Choose friends who enjoy cooking or who would like to learn more about cooking. Choose a cookery book and allocate a recipe from the book to each cookery book club member. Bring to the feast and feast!

Crafternoon club

Choose crafty friends whose skills you'd like to learn from. At the crafternoon club, members bring their unfinished items, whether a hand-sewn skirt, a knitted sweater or a beaded bracelet, and help each other to get them done over lunch.

There is very little energy that is
as strong as female camaraderie.

Books for book club

1. *Americanah*
   by Chimamanda Ngozi Adichie

2. *The Color Purple*
   by Alice Walker

3. *Eat Pray Love*
   by Elizabeth Gilbert

4. *I Know Why the Caged Bird Sings*
   by Maya Angelou

5. *The Handmaid's Tale*
   by Margaret Atwood

The Bayeux Tapestry

Visualize your land after invasion, your king killed by an arrow in the eye and 100,000 of your countrymen massacred by the marauding forces. How can women process this scale of defeat? By sewing The Bayeux Tapestry, of course. Commissioned by Norman Bishop Odo, it is believed that Anglo-Saxon women embroidered the tapestry in Kent. At nearly 70 metres/ 230 feet long, the tapestry tells the story of the death of England's King Edward the Confessor and the triumph of William the Conqueror over his successor, King Harold.

While almost nothing is known of the women whose storytelling stitches have survived for nearly 1,000 years, it requires no imagination to immediately picture the camaraderie shared around the cloth. Stitch by stich these marvellous women preserved history for all time.

The sisterhood of quilting circles

Imagine America in the 1800s and the pioneer women who handmade everything necessary to live comfortably.

Perhaps the ultimate example of the creative sisterhood, the American folk art of quilting combines utility, comradeship, craft and thrift, where memories and collective imagination are threaded within the fabric.

- Read
  Quilting for Dummies by Cheryl Fall.

- Start a quilting bee
  Begin with a group of friends sewing a small square each and combining to make a table placement.

- Watch
  How to Make an American Quilt, 1995, starring Winona Ryder about a young woman guided down the path of love by the members of her grandmother's quilting circle.

Easy, creative and communal projects:

Get together with a group of friends and spend the weekend creating a beautiful keepsake for your memories...

- Pool old clothes to quilt cushion covers together. Though individual, each cover will be a reminder of your shared sisterhood.

- Attend a pottery workshop, create a joint design and make unique cups that capture your friendship.

- Buy a canvas and acrylic paints to make a mural out of your handprints. The work may be photographed and reprinted on canvas so that everyone in the sisterhood circle has a copy.

Sisterhood soundtrack

- "Count On Me", Whitney Houston and CeCe Winans

- "Girls Just Want to Have Fun", Cyndi Lauper

- "Sisters Doin' It for Themselves", Eurythmics and Aretha Franklin

- "We Are Family", Sister Sledge

- "Run the World", Beyoncé

- "Feeling Good", Nina Simone

- "Hey, Soul Sister", Train

- "Anytime You Need a Friend", Mariah Carey

Walking with the sisterhood

In 1996, 13 bra-clad women power-walked the New York City Marathon to raise money for breast cancer. Over 20 years later, hundreds of thousands of women have participated in similar walks to raise over £100 million for breast-cancer charities.

Make a list of what you really want and need *from* the women in your life.

Make a list of what you really want and need to do *for* the women in your life.

MoonWalks

With decorated bras as the signature motif, participants walk at night in MoonWalks. Inspired to defeat rotten illnesses, MoonWalks have become magnificent festivals of female endeavour and friendship. These walks happen around the world: in England, Iceland, America, Germany, along the pilgrimage routes of Spain and even in the Arctic.

Exhalation! Triumph! Victory!

There is nothing quite like the shared highs and lows of sporting triumph and disaster. The sweat and tears of training and defeats are all forgotten in the white-hot heat of victory.

Experience the physical limits of the sisterhood by joining your local sports team.

Pick up the thread

There is never one conversation to be had with women; rather thoughts are put down, picked up and then woven into the never-ending conversation of the eternal sisterhood. It weaves through the generations and threads from woman to woman, mother to daughter, sister to sister. The topics are universal and each woman adds another stitch to the tapestry of sisterhood understanding.

Pick up the thread, ask and answer...

- Is this love?
- How do I live a good life?
- How do I stay healthy?
- What more should I be doing?
- Is this good enough?

The Vestal Virgins

Groups of women living together have historically been revered and treated almost like goddesses.

For nearly 1,000 years, the Vestal Virgins lived in esteemed isolation in Rome. Six virgins, selected between the ages of six and 10, served for 30 years near the Temple of Vesta where their sacred task was to protect the eternal fire.

Expected to live decorously, the Vestal Virgins wore flowing white gowns and ribbons, and fashioned their hair with six or seven elaborate plaits/braids. They drove around in luxury two-wheeled carriages, had reserved seats at the games, could pardon prisoners and were much sought after as wives after their 30-year stint in the temple.

Medieval convent life

While we may imagine veiled women leading a life of simple prayer, 12th-century convents across Europe were also places of education and offered women tranquillity, respect from the local community and the freedom not to marry men thrust upon them by their family. In England alone, over 100 convents with places for over 3,000 nuns were established in the 1100s.

Though there were plenty of nuns who concentrated solely on contemplation, convents were bustling affairs.

Nuns were involved in medieval business, abbesses took on particular legal roles in local towns, the nuns raised illegitimate children from highborn houses and convents were used as retirement centres for aged female aristocrats. Nuns provided charity in times of hardship as well as medical and hospitality facilities for pilgrims and travellers.

Medieval England saw convent life thrive up until Henry VIII's dissolution of the monasteries in the 16th century.

Hildegard von Bingen

Hildegard von Bingen is an inspiration for the sisterhood. Having spent most of her life cloistered with women, she wrote music that can be appreciated by all of humanity.

Enclosed in the female section of Disibodenberg monastery in Germany in the early 1100s, at the approximate age of eight, Hildegard saw visions of "the shade of the living light".

Being a sickly child, the youngest of 10 siblings, did not stop Hildegard flourishing in the religious order and going on to found two monasteries.

A polymath, Hildegard wrote three volumes of theology, the world's first morality play and some of the most exquisite music ever imagined.

The celestial harmonies written by Hildegard von Bingen convey spiritual ecstasy that is as moving now in a secular world as it was over eight centuries ago in a small Christian cloister.

A–Z of inspirational women

Ada Lovelace
Beyoncé
Chidera Eggerue
Diana Spencer
Emma Watson
Frida Kahlo
Greta Thunberg
Helen Keller
Isabel Allende
Jane Goodall
Katharine Hepburn
Lucille Ball
Marie Curie

Nora Ephron
Oprah Winfrey
Pearl S. Buck
Queen Elizabeth II
Rosa Parks
Serena Williams
Tarana Burke
Ursula Le Guin
Valentina Tereshkova
Wangari Maathai
Xue Xinran
Yuri Kochiyama
Zaha Hadid

Sorority sisters

As more women were, often reluctantly, being allowed to study at formerly male-only American universities in the late 19th century, female students often found the conditions hostile. Classes were segregated between the sexes and many clubs were off-limits for the women. It's no wonder then that these early educational pioneers joined together to form female organizations within universities and take comfort and solace in each other's company.

Gamma Phi Beta was one such society set up by four female students at Syracuse University, New York, in 1874. Thinking that "fraternity" was the wrong name for a group of women, a new name was formulated and Gamma Phi Beta was the first organization to be known as a sorority.

There are growing numbers of sororities, and while they are criticized for being elitist, exclusive and reckless in their initiation ceremonies, the notion of women banding together to help each other in lasting friendships began on solid sisterhood foundations.

" The Founders of Gamma Phi Beta were a rather serious minded group of girls. Conditions at that time made them so. They were pioneers in the matter of education and had won the privilege after much bitter opposition. Many thought women unfitted for the strenuous study of a university course, that they had neither the physique nor the brains for such an undertaking and, of course, we were anxious to prove ourselves the equals of our brothers or any other man. "

FRANCES ELIZABETH HAVEN

" *Women do feel themselves aggrieved, oppressed, and fraudulently deprived of their most sacred rights, we insist that they have immediate admission to all the rights and privileges which belong to them as citizens of these United States.*

In entering upon the great work before us, we anticipate no small amount of misconception, misrepresentation, and ridicule; but we shall use every instrumentality within our power to effect our object. "

ELIZABETH CADY STANTON
The Declaration of Sentiments

Elizabeth Cady Stanton

Be empowered by what a conversation with friends can lead to. Young mother and housewife Elizabeth Cady Stanton was enjoying tea with friends in 1848 when the conversation turned to female emancipation. The chatting soon turned to vigorous action and a fortnight later the women had organized a two-day meeting in Seneca Falls, New York, to discuss female rights. Elizabeth Cady Stanton penned the Declaration of Sentiments, which advocated rights for American woman.

She is widely regarded as the mother of women's suffrage movements in America but died 18 years before the franchise was extended to women in 1920.

10 famous sorority sisters

- **Aretha Franklin,** singer,
  Delta Sigma Theta (honorary)

- **Betty White,** actress,
  Alpha Gamma Delta

- **Cheryl Crow,** singer,
  Kappa Alpha Theta

- **Condoleezza Rice,** politician,
  Alpha Chi Omega

- **Harper Lee,** author,
  Chi Omega (honorary)

- **Kate Spade,** designer,
  Kappa Kappa Gamma

- **Kathy Bates,** actress,
  Alpha Delta Pi

- **Maya Angelou,** poet and civil
  rights activist, Alpha Kappa
  Alpha (honorary)

- **Meghan Markle,** Duchess of Sussex,
  Kappa Kappa Gamma

- **Sheryl Crawford,** broadway producer,
  Delta Gamma

Annie Minerva Turnbo Malone

The 10th of 11 children of former slaves, Annie Turnbo had no formal education. Yet she took a particular interest in chemistry at school in Illinois and founded a cosmetics enterprise for African-American women that made her one of the first black female millionaires.

Turnbo's hair-care products helped African-American women view their hair as beautiful rather than something just to be managed. Her business model of door-to-door cosmetic sales women gave work to many former slaves in need of it.

In addition, this marvellous woman established a beauty college named Poro College in 1917. She was dedicated to improving the lives of black women and the college also offered classes to prepare women for the workplace.

Sisterhood: the positive
axis of female solidarity.

Sisterhood is the comfort of knowing that even when you feel alone, you aren't.

Millicent Garrett Fawcett

Millicent Garrett Fawcett is remembered as one of the most effective suffragists in Britain, who drove the political agenda to give 8.5 million women over the age of 30 the right to vote in the 1918 Representation of the People Act.

Inspired at the age of 19 after listening to a speech by John Stuart Mill on equal voting rights, Millicent dedicated herself to the cause, becoming President of the National Union of Women's Suffrage Societies.

A serial founder, joiner and leader of political organizations, Millicent Fawcett embodied the art of creating political change within existing structures. She used the intellectual arts of persuasion and debate to change the law.

Britain's second female Prime Minister, Theresa May, unveiled a statue to Millicent Fawcett in 2018 (the centenary of female suffrage) – the first statue of a woman to stand in London's Parliament Square.

Women banding together can change the world.

"Those who write and speak against the extension of liberty of action and conscience to men and women have always said that the change they deprecate will undermine or decompose the foundations of society. A few years pass by, the change is accomplished, and it turns out that society is not undermined or decomposed at all, but is all the healthier and more vigorous, through being possessed of a larger proportion of free citizens."

MILLICENT GARRETT FAWCETT

Prunella Briance

After experiencing an excruciating
Caesarean in the middle of a power cut
and then the stillbirth of a daughter,
Prunella Briance dedicated her life
to improving women's experience
of childbirth.

Prunella placed an advert in *The Times* on 4 May 1956 stating her interest in founding a society to promote natural childbirth. She was inundated with responses from women whose experiences of childbirth had been less than pleasant. The National Childbirth Trust was founded in 1957 with the aim, "that women should be humanely treated during pregnancy and in labour, never hurried, bullied or ridiculed".

The NCT is now the largest charity for parents, with over 300 branches around the country offering ante- and post-natal classes.

Leyla Hussein OBE and Nimco Ali OBE

Leyla Hussein and Nimco Ali, both born in Somalia, founded Daughters of Eve, an anti-FGM not-for-profit organization, and were instrumental in persuading the British government to commit £50 million to eliminating FGM across Africa.

They were awarded Orders of the British Empire in the 2019 HM The Queen's Birthday Honours List.

In their friendship and shared experience, they bound together in work to save millions of girls, born and unborn, from suffering their fate.

When women support each other,
incredible things happen.

Ways to help the sisterhood grow:

- Exposure
- Support
- Community

Angeline Murimirwa

Angeline Murimirwa was not one of over 50 million girls of school age who are denied an education in sub-Saharan Africa. Instead, she was one of the first girls from Zimbabwe to receive a grant from CAMFED (Campaign for Female Education) to attend school and has since risen to become CAMFED's Executive Director in Africa. Angeline is passionate about sharing the chances she had with other girls of rural Africa.

Angeline concentrates on finding local solutions to encourage female education, knowing the positive changes that educating girls can bring.

CAMFED now supports over 6,000 partner schools for girls in Zimbabwe, Zambia, Ghana, Tanzania and Malawi, over 3 million girls at primary school and over 900,000 young women at secondary school.

Pulitzer Prize-winning novelists Sheryl WuDunn and Nicholas Kristoff featured Angeline in their book *Half the Sky*.

You can tell who the strong women are. They are the ones building each other up rather than tearing each other down.

The progress of women's rights has no doubt come a long way, but we still have a long way to go to address injustice in:

- Child marriage
- Domestic violence
- FGM
- The gender pay gap
- Lack of education
- Period poverty
- Rape
- Reproductive health

Suhani Jalota

With over 320 million women in India
without access to sanitary pads, and
menstruation still treated as taboo,
Suhani Jalota has dedicated her life
to improving menstruation hygiene
and employing women in the process.
As founder and CEO of the Myna
Mahila Foundation, Suhani is on a
mission to provide affordable sanitary
napkins, generate female employment
in slums and build women's networks.
So far, over half a million pads have
been made by women and over 3,000
women who previously used rags are
using the products.

The foundation is one of only seven chosen to benefit from donations marking the wedding of Prince Harry and Meghan Markle.

The impressive and compassionate Suhani was honoured with Forbes 30 Under 30 Asia 2018, and named one of *Glamour*'s College Women of the Year 2016 and a Queen's Young Leader in 2017 representing India.

Malala Yousafzai

Shot in the head aged 15 by the Taliban for going to school in the Swat District of Pakistan, Malala Yousafzai recovered to become a global leader for girls' education.

Born in 1997, Malala blogged about her experiences of life under the Taliban for BBC Urdu and was nominated for the International Children's Peace Prize.

After taking an exam and being shot at while travelling home on a bus, Malala's survival and refusal to be cowed led to immediate global acclaim for her courage and stance on education. She was co-recipient of the Nobel Peace Prize in 2014.

Malala's activism continues with the establishment of the Malala Fund. The international organization fights for girls' education and aims to ensure 12 years of free, safe and good-quality education for every girl in the world.

What a woman. How lucky the sisterhood is to have Malala among its number.

"I don't want to be remembered as the girl who was shot. I want to be remembered as the girl who stood up."

MALALA YOUSAFZAI

" The perfect woman, you see was a working woman; not an idler; not a fine lady; but one who used her hands and her head and her heart for the good of others."

THOMAS HARDY

Remember

Trying to be a man is
a waste of a woman.

*"Alone we can do so little;
together we can do so much."*

HELEN KELLER

Understand that:

- The sisterhood at work does not mean harmful competition.

- Becoming part of a sisterhood of businesswomen at work will enhance your self-confidence.

- Making an effort with women at work will boost both your personal and professional life.

Who wouldn't want a group of competent women on their side?

Try not to resent women at work who are at different life stages to you. Remember, life is not static and you will undoubtedly experience differing roles within your working lifetime that will all require the support of the sisterhood.

Try to get along with women of all the different types of female work personalities...

- Gossiper
- Comedian
- Junior
- Senior
- Inbetweener
- Sharer
- Part-timer
- Desk-eater
- Complainer
- Newbie

Success at work does not mean modelling masculine behaviour. Don't be afraid to employ the feminine side of your character in the workspace.

Care-giving/nurturing/compassion are just as important as assertiveness and directness.

Create environments where other women feel happy to bring the female side of their character to the office.

Empathy and intuition are just as useful as competitiveness.

Create time to reflect and carefully consider decisions, and encourage others to harness the business power of instinct.

Debbie Wosskow OBE

Meet Debbie Wosskow, an entrepreneur who, after selling her business Love Home Swap for $53 million, has dedicated herself to furthering women in business. Her latest venture, the AllBright Collective, is a platform that provides capital, skills and networks to female business founders. With 800 founder members, AllBright Collective is pioneering the trend for more female-only networking business spaces.

She was awarded an OBE in 2016 for services to business.

Get involved with the sisterhood at work:

1. Ask the HR department about female–female mentoring schemes.

2. Join relevant female-only groups at work.

3. Find a female ally.

4. Attend professional female-only networking events, conferences and symposiums.

Keep up with the Kardashians

The high priestesses of the modern-day business sisterhood have to be the Kardashian sisters whose net worth ranks in the billions.

Having mastered the art of branding and bottoms, The Kardashian sisters Kourtney, Kim, Khloe, Kendall and Kylie have displayed awesome business skills, selling not only their looks and family drama, but millions of dollars' worth of makeup.

There is strength in sisterhood.

Verónica Caridad Rabelo, Assistant Professor of Management in the College of Business at San Francisco State University, speaks eloquently about how to utilize the sisterhood in the workspace. She emphasizes that the sisterhood doesn't mean women are "the same", nor that female struggles are "the same" or indeed that women have to "like each other". She insists rather that sisterhood struggles are "interconnected" and women should learn from each other's experiences and not "throw each other under the bus".

Empowered women empower women.

Brilliant books written by brilliant women

- *Lean In: Women, Work and the Will to Lead* by Sheryl Sandberg

- *Little Black Book: A Toolkit for Working Women* by Otegha Uwagba

- *Moment of Lift: How Empowering Women Changes the World* by Melinda Gates

- *The Path Made Clear: Discovering Your Life's Direction and Purpose* by Oprah Winfrey

- *Thrive: The Third Metric to Redefining Success and Creating a Happier Life* by Arianna Huffington

- *Wolfpack: How to Come Together, Unleash Our Power and Change the Game* by Abby Wambach

Model supportive sisterhood behaviour in the workplace

In an interview with BBC Radio 4's *Woman's Hour*, Melinda Gates demonstrated how being the working wife of Bill Gates, the boss of Microsoft, empowered her to evaluate equality within the home and workplace.

Melinda Gates spoke passionately about modelling supportive behaviour and how she and Bill constantly questioned their roles as care-givers. They agreed to equalize family responsibilities, and when other wives saw Bill Gates driving his daughter to school several days a week, they in turn encouraged their husbands to become more hands-on.

Never underestimate how many women in the workplace will look to you for inspiration.

QUOTES ARE TAKEN FROM

Bindu: Contemporary actress in Indian cinema

Charlotte Brontë: 19th-century author of
Jane Eyre

Christina Rossetti: 19th-century poet and Pre-Raphaelite muse

Queen Elizabeth I: English 16th-century monarch

Elizabeth Cady Stanton: 19th-century American
suffragist, social activist and abolitionist

Emily Dickinson: 19th-century American poet

Frances Elizabeth Haven: One of the four founders
of Gamma Phi Beta, the first university society for
women known as a sorority

George Eliot: 19th-century English author
of *Middlemarch*

Helen Keller: Deaf and dumb educator

Käthe Kollwitz: 20th-century German artist

Katherine Mansfield: Early 20th-century
New Zealand writer

Lady Mary Wortley Montagu: 18th-century English letter writer and poet

Leo Tolstoy: 19th-century Russian author of *War and Peace*

Louisa May Alcott: 19th-century American author of *Little Women*

Malala Yousafzai: Pakistani activist for education and Nobel laureate

Mary Wollstonecraft: 18th-century writer and proto-feminist

Millicent Garrett Fawcett: 19th–20th century suffragist

Thomas Hardy: 19th-century English author

Thucydides: Ancient Greek historian

Verónica Caridad Rabelo: Assistant Professor of Management in the College of Business at San Francisco State University

William Cobbett: 18th-century English pamphleteer

FURTHER READING

A Secret Sisterhood: The Hidden Friendships of Austen, Brontë, Eliot and Woolf, by Emily Midorikawa and Emma Claire Sweeney, Aurum Press

Becoming by Michelle Obama, Viking

The Bell Jar by Sylvia Plath, Faber & Faber

Brief Lives: 150 Intimate Biographies of the Famous by the Famous, Oxford University Press

Chambers Dictionary of World History, Chambers

Complete Stories by Dorothy Parker, Penguin Books

Medieval women, a social history of women in England 450-1500 by Henrietta Leyser, Phoenix Giant

Outrageous Acts and Everyday Rebellions by Gloria Steinem, Picador

Oxford Dictionary of Nursery Rhymes edited by Iona and Peter Opie, Oxford University Press

The Oxford Dictionary of Quotations, Oxford University Press

The Sacred and the Feminine in Ancient Greece edited by Sue Blundell and Margaret Williamson, Routledge

The Second Shift by Arlie Russell Hochschild with Anne Machung, Penguin Books

USEFUL WEBSITES

ancestry.com

babble.com

basketballengland.co.uk

camfed.org

englandhockey.co.uk

englandlacrosse.co.uk

englandnetball.co.uk

englandrugby.com/england/senior-women

gal-dem.com

malala.org

manrepeller.com

mumsnet.com

mynamahila.com

nationalquilterscircle.com

nct.org.uk

oprah.com

skillshare.com

thefa.com/womens-girls-football

theglasshammer.com

thewi.org.uk

walkthewalk.org

Publishing Director Sarah Lavelle
Editor Harriet Webster
Assistant Editor Stacey Cleworth
Words Joanna Gray
Series Designer Emily Lapworth
Junior Designer Alicia House
Production Director Stephen Lang
Production Controller Sinead Hering

Published in 2019 by Quadrille,
an imprint of Hardie Grant
Publishing

Quadrille
52–54 Southwark Street
London SE1 1UN
quadrille.com

The publisher has made every
effort to trace the copyright
holders. We apologize in advance
for any unintentional omissions
and would be pleased to insert the
appropriate acknowledgement in
any subsequent edition.

Cataloguing in Publication Data:
a catalogue record for this book is
available from the British Library.

ISBN 978 1 78713 518 5

Printed in China